UPON
A
PILLOW
AF278847

Mariah Debra
Gale Messinger

Dedicated to

My incredible children

Craig & Jenn

Who were,

are

and will always be

my Muses

About the Author

Mariah Debra Gale Messinger is the mother of boy/girl twins.

In her travels, she has lived in New Jersey, Washington DC, the Blue Ridge Mountains of Virginia, Santa Cruz, CA, the wilderness of Wolf Creek, OR and then finally settled in San Francisco, CA.

It was in Afton, VA, in the Blue Ridge Mountains, that she began writing and illustrating children's books. First, for her twins delight and then because the stories would not stop coming out of her!

At this time, Mariah is Owner/Director/Head Teacher of a home based Pre-school, Pre-K, Daycare. Children are and have always been an integral part of her life. This book was inspired by her own experience, albeit, just one of many...

Pillows are soft
like fur
like velvet

They are good for cuddling
like a ferret
like a stuffed animal pet

You can hold them
hug them
toss them
throw them
sit on them

Pillow fights
with your friends
are fun

Just don't hit
too hard
you might
hurt someone

like your mom.

Pillows are soft
    for plopping on
        like in front of the TV
        like on the floor
        with a
            favorite book

Pillows are
blue
and green
and more

You can buy any color
                shape or
                size
                    at the store

← SMALL PILLOWS
BIG PILLOWS →
THE PILLOW STORE
SALE

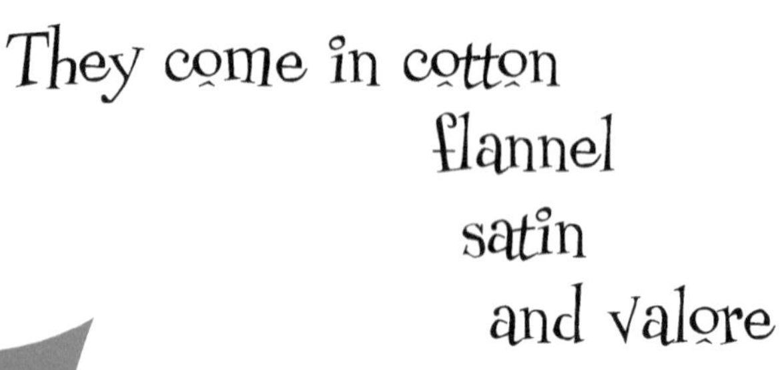

They come in cotton
flannel
satin
and valore

Each
Its` sole purpose
to comfort
the needy
with softness galore

You can punch one
when you're mad

AAH!
ARRG!

Cry into one
when you're sad

BOO HOO
SIGH!
HEAVE!
MOAN!

You can prop
your head
high
with one

Or hide
it
inside
of some

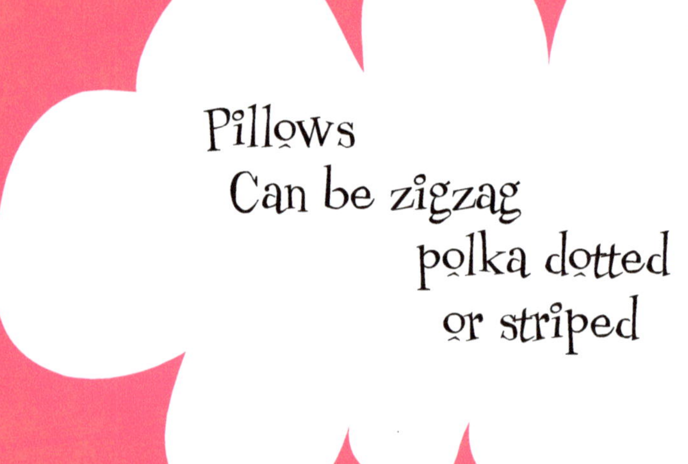
Pillows
Can be zigzag
polka dotted
or striped

Some tasseled
some laced

Little pillows
for this

Big pillows
for that

Some slender
some squat

Pillows
    quite happily
    shaped
      like a cat

And
best of all

Pillows are soft
for laying
your head upon
your head upon

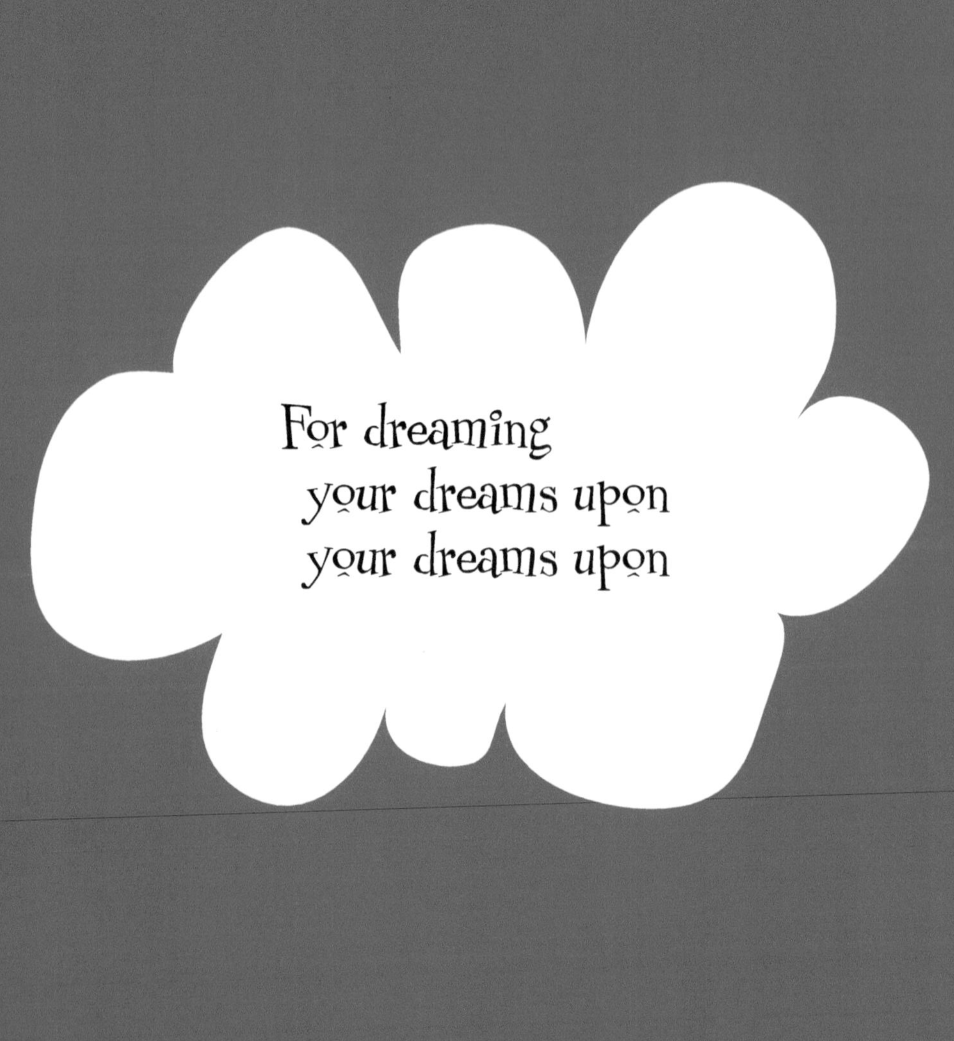

For dreaming
your dreams upon
your dreams upon

Goodnight Sweet dreams

Parents & Pre-school Teachers

Upon a Pillow Games:

1) Each child holds a pillow, any pillow. As the parent or teacher
reads the story, each child acts out each page.
For instance, " You can hold them, hug them, toss them, throw
them, sit on them". Child does each of these things with the
pillow.
At the end of the story, each child lays his or her head down on
the pillow to pretend sleep.
For bedtime each child lays his or her head down to really
sleep.

2) Count the pillows on each page.

3) Name the colors, shapes, textures and designs of the pillows on
each page.

To add to the learning process you can make an:
Upon a Pillow Swatch Book
Upon a Pillow Pillow

Make a Swatch Book!

You will need:

4 x 4" Swatches of each fabric and pattern mentioned in the story.

Poster board

Scissors

School glue

Hole punch

A 6 inch snap chain from the hardware store

1) Cut 5 x 5" squares from the poster board.

2) Glue the fabric squares onto the poster board squares.

3) Punch a hole in the top left hand corner of each square.

4) Run snap chain through all holes and snap shut.

You now have an Upon a Pillow Swatch Book!

Make a Pillow!
You will need:

Larger amounts of each fabric and pattern (or pick one or a few)

Sewing machine or needle and thread

Scissors

Pillow stuffing

Cut two of the same shapes of each fabric and pattern into any size or shape.

1) Cut two of the same shapes of each fabric and pattern into any size or shape.

2) Place shapes front to front

3) Sew around 3/4 of the shape, leaving an opening for the stuffing

4) Turn right sides out

5) Stuff with pillow stuffing to desired plumpness

6) Turn unsewn part in to match already sewn sides and finish sewing with needle and thread

You now have an Upon a Pillow Pillow!

Encourage children to touch each fabric (texture) and trace the patterns on the Swatch Book or Pillows. Then match them to the page and words in the story.